THE ROYAL NAVY AT CHATHAM
1900 - 2000
by John Whatling

HMS Springer seen here at Chatham Navy Days 1957. Launched by Cammell Laird on 14 May 1945, these small patrol submarines of the S class, once in service, proved extremely capable and were built in large numbers over a 15 year period (eleven of them built at Chatham alone). Shortly after this photo was taken she was sold to Israel and renamed **Tannin** (note the "snort" in its stowed position on the after casing). Beyond **Springer** is berthed the Battle class destroyer **Lagos**.   (Bill Rice)

Author's Notes

I would like to thank the following for their help in the preparation of this book, for without it I could never have completed the project.

All the friends at Chatham Dockyard Historical Society especially to Harold Bennett to whom nothing was too much trouble during my numerous visits, answering questions providing the vast majority of the photographs and helping with the research. Their dedication to preserving the History of the Dockyard is second to none.

To Mike Critchley and Steve Bush of Maritime Books for their advice, guidance and most of all patience with a very novice author. Also thanks to Ben Warlow for casting his expert eye over the manuscript and enhancing many of the captions.

I have made every effort to verify names and dates, there may be slight errors and I apologise for these in advance and hope that your enjoyment is not otherwise spoiled.

John Whatling.
August 2003

The Royal Navy at Chatham 1900 - 2000

The Chatham Naval Base consisted of two main parts, the Dockyard and **HMS Pembroke** (the Barracks), both under the command of the Commander-in-Chief Nore.

But how did it all begin?

Chatham, lying in a bend of the River Medway had grown slowly from a small settlement into a village relying on agriculture and fishing for its livelihood. The site had seen some small-scale boat building, then in 1488 the **Grace Dieu** was built, the first two decker custom built for the Royal Navy, which, until this time had a fleet composed of merchant ships converted in war-time to the carrying of The Kings Men.

It was possibly the building of this ship in such an unknown place as Chatham, that the "powers to be" suddenly became interested in this quite corner of Kent. The Admiralty promoted some interest in Chatham becoming a base for the Navy. England at this time seemed to be in a perpetual state of war with our neighbours across the Channel. An anchorage was required for the fleet which would also give protection to the Medway and the Thames.

The port was far enough up the river to be easily defended and the surrounding hills gave protection from the winter storms. The muddy bottom of the river coupled with its high rise and fall of the tide allowed ships to be careened (enabling their ships bottoms to be cleaned and recaulked) with ease. So Chatham become an anchorage for naval ships in the reign of King Henry VIII.

Thus grew the Royal Naval Dockyard Chatham. 500 acres of docks. Slipways, ship building facilities and all the bits and pieces that go with it. Shipwrights shops. ropery, sail lofts, boilermakers and engineering facilities. With its three large basins the dockyard had facilities to both build and repair most ships in the Navy. Building every class of ship from the **Grace Dieu** through **HMS Victory** to the submarine **HMS Ocelot** - the last RN warship to be built at Chatham, and repairing the same through every major conflict over the last 400 years - right up to the Cod Wars.

The first naval Depot was established at Chatham in 1890, the men living in hulks in number two basin. A former flagship of The C-in-C Nore **HMS Duncan** was renamed **HMS Pembroke** in 1890 and accommodated the officers, seaman and Engine Room Artificers. All the remainder lived aboard **HMS Royal Adelaide** and **HMS Forte**. **HMS Algiers** served as quarters for the Captain and Staff of the Dockyard Reserves and an old cruiser **HMS Warspite** provided overflow accommodation. The Naval Depot proper consisted of **HM Ships Pembroke, Royal Adelaide** and **Forte**. It soon became obvious that they were totally unsuited for this purpose and so the Admiralty decided to build a Naval barracks ashore.

On 30 April 1903, led by the Depot Band, 5,000 officers and men from the hulks left the Dockyard by Pembroke Gate marched along Dockyard Road into the Barracks by the Main Gate. The main buildings had been completed in 1902 but not used until this time. Over the next few years the following the Commodore's House, St George's Church and the gymnasium were added.

In 1914 East Camp was built to accommodate the large number of men the Fleet required in wartime. North Camp was completed in 1917. Even so men were still sleeping in the Drill Shed when on the night of 3 September 1917, two bombs from a German airplane scored direct hits killing 135 ratings and wounding many more. After the First World War East Camp was demolished, a new camp not being built until 1938.

Again with the outbreak of the Second World War such was the increase of numbers drafted in to man the ships and Dockyard facilities that outlying accommodation was utilised. St Mary's Barracks was taken over in August 1941 and occupied by personnel from the Gunnery School. Additionally, tunnels that had been constructed as air raid shelters were used as living areas.

HMS Pembroke survived the war years and was very little changed during the late 40's and early 50's. It was at **Pembroke** that the Royal Guards for the Coronation were trained alongside the guards for the 50th Anniversary of **HMS Pembroke** celebrations in 1953. In March 1958 the drill staff from the Gunnery School trained the guard from **HMS Paladin** prior to the ships visit to Zeebrugge for the 40th anniversary of the raid to block that port on the night of April 22/23 1918.

After the war ended Chatham, along with the other ports, was soon gearing up for the re-opening of the Royal Tournament. Her Field Gun teams were soon breaking records. Alas all was to be short lived. In 1959 the Gunnery School was closed and replaced by the Supply School which was being relocated from **HMS Ceres** at Wetherby in Yorkshire. The saddest thing of all that was to darken **Pembroke's** all too short existence was considered to be the closing of the Chatham Depot with the introduction of Centralised Drafting - and the loss of the title "The Royal Naval Barracks". This was followed by the handing over of large parts of the Barracks to the Dockyard including the Commodore's House, Drill Shed, and part of the Parade Ground all being surplus to requirements. The next to go was the title C-in-C the Nore as the senior officers post was downgraded to Flag Officer Medway. The post of Commodore ceased in March 1961 and the Captain of the Supply School assumed the command of **HMS Pembroke**.

It was in June 1981 that the final nail was knocked home into **Pembroke's** coffin. The Defence Review of that year decreed that **HMS Pembroke** together with the rest of the Naval Base, would close on 31 March 1984 just 81 years after it opened.

Today what remains of the site is now a tourist attraction consisting of the remaining dockyard buildings, a museum, the preserved destroyer **Cavalier**, submarine **Ocelot** and the sloop **Gannet**.

This photograph, taken in 1902, shows the original Chatham Naval Depot - **HMS Pembroke**. Opened in 1890 to accommodate the reserve fleet and to provide training facilities for men waiting to be drafted to ships. The three hulks are from right to left **HMS Forte** (3rd rate 74 gun screw ship formerly **HMS Pembroke**), **HMS Adelaide** (1st rate) and **HMS Pembroke** (formerly **HMS Duncan** Flagship C-in-C Nore). Over 5,000 men, officers, seamen, engineers, artificers and marines were accommodated in these ships - a situation that proved inadequate for the purpose and led to the building of the new barracks in 1902.

After the trials and tribulations of living in the hulks for so long, Jack naturally felt a little strange in his new surroundings but he quickly acclimatised himself to this new found luxury. The new blocks were named after the Royal Navy's most famous Admirals - Anson, Blake, Duncan, Grenville, Hawke and Nelson. Each barrack room consisted of 12 messes of 14 men. Each mess had a table and two stools and its own mess traps, and (as at sea) this was where the sailor took his meals, had his recreation and slept. A new innovation - that of electric light - though of low power output made an immense improvement from the oil lamps of the hulks.

HMS Empress of India was laid down in 1889 and completed in 1893. One of eight Royal Sovereign Class Battleships she had a very short life span, being sunk as a target ship in the Channel in 1913. She was sorely missed when WW1 started less than a year later. Here she is seen during refit in 1902 in No.8 Dock. Only the last of the class, ***Hood***, had the twin 13.5 inch guns mounted in turrets instead of the open barbettes - as can be seen here.

The turn of the century still found wooden walled ships undergoing repairs in the Dockyard. This early photograph shows **HMS Achilles** in No 2 Dock. **Achilles** was the biggest steam warship in the world when floated out at Chatham in 1863 and the first ironbuilt warship to be constructed in a Royal Dockyard. The only RN warship to step 4 masts (reduced to three in 1865) she carried a full complement of sail - a total of 50,000 square feet of canvas when fully rigged. The preserved clipper **Cutty Sark**, as a comparison, carried 30,000 square feet. **Achilles** was used as a depot ship at Chatham under the names **Egremont** and **Pembroke** from 1914 until she was broken up in 1923.

Both the last and the largest battleship to be built at Chatham, **HMS Africa** is seen at her launching on 20 May 1905, becoming the first vessel launched from No8 slip. Seven years later she made history when Lt. Samsom RN made the epic first flight from a Royal Naval ship in a Shorts S27. Chatham Dockyard built a ramp from the fore turret to the bow for the trial flight. Though successful, traditionalists were not happy as the flightdeck made her forward 12-inch guns unusable. The *Africa* paid off in February 1919 and was sold to Ellis of Newcastle in 1920 for breaking up.

The Dockyard Church, which is situated just inside the Main Gate was built by Dockyard Craftsmen in 1811. From its completion until closure it served as the religious centre for the men working within the Dockyard. Weddings, christenings and funerals were conducted over the years and it is said that there were many who took part in all three services. Today the Church is no longer consecrated as such and stands a silent reminder to all those who have passed through its doors. The figurehead is from *HMS Wellesley* (1812).

Chatham Naval Base has always echoed to the sound of music. This photograph, taken in 1903 shows the original Blue Jacket Band and the Royal Marine practicing on the main road. The bands have, over the years, played for Royalty, VIP's and many Ceremonial Parades up to the 1960's.

The first ceremonial Divisions held at **Pembroke** gives some idea of how many sailors and marines were accommodated in the barracks in those early days. Compare this with the photograph of the final ceremonial Divisions on page 98.

HMS Irresistible seen here at her launching at Chatham on 15 December 1898. One of three Formidable Class vessels laid down in 1898 at each of the major dockyards. These battleships of 15,000 tons were armed with four 12-inch and twelve 6-inch guns. She had a speed of 18 knots. A mine off Gallipoli sank her in March 1915. The boatmen are waiting to collect the tallow from the slipway, which they then sold back to the yards.

HMS Tartar is seen here in June 1917 in No. 8 Dock undergoing repairs after her bows were damaged by a mine whilst on Dover Patrol.

Launched in 1907, she was the first destroyer built at Woolston, Southampton. This damage was caused after hitting a mine whilst escorting paddle minesweepers near the Gravelines Buoy on 24 June, she having reportedly steered the wrong side of a marker buoy.

Stranger than fiction.... On 27 October 1916 the destroyer **HMS Nubian** was struck forward by a German torpedo, severing the forward one third of the ship. However, she refused to sink and was taken in tow by the **William Gray**, but the wind strength increased and the crippled warship was blown onto the South Foreland rocks. The ship was almost abandoned, being hard up against the base of the cliffs, but, after many weeks of hard work she was refloated and towed to Dover.....

......On 8 November 1916, her sistership, **HMS Zulu**, had struck a mine which caused the after end of the ship to break away. The remaining part was towed to Calais by the French destroyer *Capitaine Mehl*. With a serviceable front section of one destroyer and a serviceable stern of another, the decision was made to create one vessel. Both vessels were towed to Chatham where on 26 April 1917 they were docked in No. 7 Dock; the mammoth task of joining the two ships together began. Completed on 7 June 1917 the new vessel was undocked and named **HMS Zubian**. Rejoining the Dover Patrol she went back into action, sinking a German submarine (*UC-50*) on 4 February 1918. She was sold in 1919.

Of all the submarines built at Chatham *X1* was the most interesting. Her design was influenced by the German submarine cruisers of WW1. Displacing 3,050 tons and armed with four 5.2 guns she was the heaviest in all respects of any submarine of her time. Laid down in November 1921 she took over three years to build. Commissioned for trials in June 1924 they took until September 1925 to complete due to problems with her machinery. She eventually joined the 1st S/M Flotilla in the eastern Mediterranean in 1926. After being slightly damaged by an internal explosion in July 1929 she returned to the UK in 1930 and paid off into reserve at Chatham for repairs to her unsatisfactory machinery. During post refit trials in February 1931 an explosion in her port engine injured 12 of her crew. After repairs *X1* commissioned for service with the 5th S/M Flotilla at Gosport. During docking in June of that year she fell against 15 Dock wall and was badly damaged. Never properly repaired she was listed for disposal and eventually broken up at Ward's in December 1936.

HMS Vindictive was laid down at Harland & Wolff and launched on 17 January 1918 as **Cavendish** - a heavy cruiser of the Improved Birmingham Class. At this time aircraft carrier trials with **HMS Furious** convinced the Admiralty of the need for more carrier type ships. She was completed on 15 October 1918 as an aircraft carrier by the removal of three of her heavy guns which were replaced by "landing and take off decks" fore and aft. On commissioning in June 1919 she was attached to the Flying Squadron, Grand Fleet. The end of the year saw her in the Baltic were she ran aground and was badly damaged. She continued carrier duties in a limited way until 1923 by which time the Admiralty had conceded the need for flight decks and island bridges. Paid off at Chatham in March 1923 she was reconverted to a cruiser. She was employed as a training ship and later as a depot repair ship. On 24 January 1946 she was sold and broken up at Blyth in February 1946.

HMS Oberon, seen here during her trials in the Medway, was laid down at Chatham as submarine **O 1** in 1924, the name was changed prior to her launching in 1926, becoming the first Royal Navy submarine to carry a name under the new policy of 1926. She spent most of her life in UK based squadrons including her war service, during which she was employed primarily as a training submarine. She was the prototype of the subsequent O Class, being recognisable from her later half sisters by her blunt "bull nose" bow. She was scrapped at Dunston in 1945.

A total of 56 submarines were built at Chatham many returning during their careers for refits and modernisation. Seen here, however, are the Vickers-built **L11** and **L25** during the first Navy Days in 1929. The "L" class submarines were of 890 to 960 tons displacement and carried one or two 4-inch guns and four or six torpedo tubes. Laid down in World War One, the majority had been scrapped by 1939. **L11** was sold in 1932 and **L25** in 1935. The cruiser ahead of **L25** is **HMS Curacoa** which was tragically lost in 1942 after a collision with **RMS Queen Mary**.

Many of the ships built in Chatham's early years were great ships of the line such as **HMS Victory**. When iron superceded wood as the main construction material and steam replaced sail, many of the skills were thought to have been lost. The Dockyard proved this was not so when, for the first Navy Days in 1929, they built this scale model of the third rate **HMS Kent** (1762).

HMS/M Sturgeon was one of eleven S class submarines built at Chatham, being launched on 8 January 1932. A member of the 6th Flotilla until 1939, she spent the next 3 years based at Blyth, Gosport and the Clyde. On 20 November 1939, she attacked and sank the German A/S trawler **V209** off Heligoland, marking the first successful Royal Naval submarine attack of the war. In 1942 she was detached to the Mediterranean returning to the UK in 1943 for a refit, during which she was transferred to the Royal Netherlands Navy and renamed **Zeehond**. She returned to the RN in 1945 and was scrapped in 1947.

The need to rapidly make safe an exposed harbour or anchorage led to the construction of two netlayers, designed to carry, lay and retrieve a net boom defence system. The first of these, **HMS Guardian** was laid down at Chatham on 15 October 1931 and launched in September 1932. Commissioned in June 1933 she joined the Home Fleet Target Service as a special trials and photographic ship for the fleet. She was detached to the Mediterranean in 1936 during the Abbysinnian Crisis. Most of her Second World War service (1941-45) was spent alternating between Malta and Oran, followed by a short period in the Far East with the British Pacific Fleet. She was placed in reserve between 1947-61, arriving at Troon for scrapping in 1962.

HMS Dundee was built as an escort sloop at Chatham in 1933. Her first two commissions were spent on the American station. In 1938 she returned to Portsmouth for a refit in which her bridge and armament were modified. On completion she recommissioned for service in the West Indies. Whilst enroute she ran aground in the St. Lawrence River on 20 September 1938. She was floated off after five days with only minor damage. She spent 1939/40 on blockade patrols searching for German merchant ships before taking over ocean escort duties. On 15 September 1940 she was torpedoed and sunk by **U-48** in the North Atlantic while escorting convoy SC.3.

In spite of heavy rain a large crowd witnessed the launching of the cruiser **HMS Arethusa**. Laid down on 25 January 1933, she was launched on 6 March 1934. Lady Tyrwhitt, wife of Admiral Sir Reginald Tyrwhitt carried out the ceremony. In May 1935 the ship arrived in the Mediterranean to become Flagship of the 3rd Cruiser Squadron. She remained until February 1940 when she transferred to the Home Fleet and the 2nd Cruiser Squadron. A refit at Chatham at the latter end of 1940 followed. She once again transferred to the Mediterranean in 1942 joining the 15th Cruiser Squadron. Hit by an aerial torpedo off the coast of North Africa she sustained substantial damage forward, being towed back to Alexandria by two destroyers......

......there she underwent temporary repairs prior to sailing to Charleston, USA, for more permanent repairs - a job that took over twelve months. By January 1944 she was once again at Chatham for a short refit. She then saw further service with the Home Fleet and the 1st Cruiser Squadron. She sustained further damage from air attack and ended the war in the Mediterranean, once again as part of the 15th Cruiser Squadron. She was reduced to reserve at Chatham in 1945 and eventually sold for scrap in 1950.

The Grimsby class sloop *HMS Deptford* at her launch on 5 February 1935 from No.4 Dock, having been named by Mrs Pearson, Mayor of the London Borough of Deptford. Shortly after commissioning she visited her London Borough namesake before sailing to the Persian Gulf. It would be over four years before she returned to the UK, arriving at Portsmouth in November 1939, where she was prepared for war duties. She helped sink *U-567* on 21 December 1941 off the Azores whilst escorting convoy HG 76. The Borough of Deptford adopted the ship during Warship Week in 1942. She served throughout the war and arrived at Cardiff in June 1945 to destore. She was placed in reserve at Milford Haven, eventually being scrapped there in March 1948.

HMS Marshall Soult was launched in 1915 as **M 14**, one of 18 Monitors built around this period. Her sister ship **Marshall Ney** was considered a failure but the lessons learnt were applied to later versions **Erebus** and **Terror**. **Marshall Soult** was used as a coastal battery vessel mainly along the Belgian coast during WW1. After the war she was used as a Turret Drill Ship at Chatham. The 15-inch guns from **Soult** and **Ney** were later fitted to **Abercrombie** and **Roberts** in 1942. The photograph shows **Marshall Soult** in 3 Basin in July 1936. The ships alongside are three V Class destroyers of WW1 vintage, inboard is **Velox**.

This photo taken during the summer of 1936 shows an unknown ships company exercising the ships landing party. From the equipment being carried they were probably conducting some form of "Aid to the Civil Power" drill. The ship in the background is the cruiser **HMS York**, one of the last pair of heavy cruisers built for the Royal Navy. She was lost in the fierce fighting for Crete in May 1941.

HMS Kellett was built in 1919 by Simons & Co. as **HMS Uppingham**, a minesweeping sloop. She was one of six Aberdare class sloops, surplus to the fleet's post war requirements, secured for conversion to Home Waters surveying vessels (in the event only 4 were completed for the RN). Conversion took place at Chatham and she was renamed **Kellett**. In 1939 she was converted back to a minesweeper at Chatham. She made 5 trips during the Dunkirk evacuation in 1940. She herself was mined in 1945 and was then scrapped.

The Dockyard, like her charges at sea, was not immune to enemy action. This photograph taken in 1942 shows the bomb damage to No. 9 Compressor House. The pumping station next door received minor damage in the same raid. Nevertheless the work of the dockyard continued unabated.

The Modified Black Swan class sloops **HM Ships _Modeste_** and **_Nereide_** (the last sloops built at Chatham) photographed at their dual launch on 29 January 1944. Specifically ordered for escort duties, both had considerable AA armament, however they were completed too late to see war service. **_Modeste_** completed at Chatham in September 1945, but was initially placed in reserve and did not commission until February 1946. She spent time in the Portsmouth Reserve Fleet (1950-52), Far East ('53) and Mediterranean ('56). In 1958 she was placed in reserve at Portsmouth before being broken up in 1961 at St David's-on-Forth. **_Nereide_** commissioned in 1946 and spent periods in the West Indies with the 7th Frigate Squadron ('53) before being placed in reserve in 1955. She was broken up at Bo'Ness in May 1958.

A further photograph of **HMS Nereide**, lying at H berth in the River Medway shortly after her commissioning. This berth was usually used for ammunitioning and compass swinging. Her heavy AA armament comprised 6 x 4-inch QF on twin mountings (two fwd, 1 aft) and 6 x 40mm Bofors (two twin and two single). She also carried Hedgehog anti-submarine mortars and depth charges. With a speed of 20 knots and a range of 7,500 miles at 12 knots, these 1,350 ton vessels proved very effective in a variety of roles. She was reclassified as a frigate in 1947.

Launched on 18 August 1944 the submarine **HMS Scotsman** is photographed in October 1947 undergoing refit to serve as a trials vessel. Much of the casing between the conning tower and bow was removed together with her gun to produce a more streamlined shape. Her engines were replaced with a unit from an A class submarine and an electric motor from a U class boat, enabling her to undertake high speed dashes. In the Spring of 1964 she was sunk off the Isle of Bute for salvage trials prior to being sold for scrapping.

HMS Dampier was built in Smiths Dock at a time when shipbuilding was at its busiest. Originally to have been the anti-submarine frigate **Loch Eil**, she was later planned to be an AA frigate, **Herne Bay**. With the end of the war, she was allocated as a survey vessel, and was completed at Chatham in June 1948, as such, being renamed **Dampier**. She was mainly employed on surveying duties in the Far East. She left Singapore on 5 October 1967 to pay off, after 19 years continuously surveying on the Far East station.

The launch cradle used for the A class submarine *HMS Acheron* in No 5 Dock just after her floating out on 27 March 1947. Intended for service in the Pacific War, where the greater distances involved required a submarine with a highersurface speed and greater endurance, none of the projected 46 vessels were completed in time to see war service. In the event only 16 were completed, *Acheron*, being the only Chatham built example. Two cruisers can be seen in the basin beyond the dock, the right hand vessel is the *Superb* (page 45) and the left hand ship is *Achilles* (page 36) which was about to refit prior to her transfer to the Royal Indian Navy.

HMS Achilles seen here in June 1948 came to public notice in December 1939, when, together with **Exeter** and **Ajax**, at the Battle of the River Plate, she pitted her 6-inch guns against the heavier 11-inch armament of the German **Admiral Graf Spee**. Serving with the New Zealand Division of the Royal Navy she returned to New Zealand and after repairs spent the rest of the war in that theatre of operations. She eventually returned to the UK in 1946. In 1950 she was sold to India and renamed **Delhi**, finally paying off in 1977.

The Ropery. The original rope house was built in 1621 and was replaced by today's building in 1780 though some parts of the current building go back to 1728. The ropery was the last one operational in the four Royal Dockyards.

Each yard identified its rope by placing a coloured "rogues yarn" in the lay. The length of these buildings (nearly a third of a mile) can be seen in these photographs.

The cruiser **HMS London** photographed at Sheerness on her return from the China station on 6 September 1949. Whilst on station she took part in the **Amethyst** rescue in April of that year. Hit 23 times by Chinese artillery as she made her dash along the Yangtse, she sustained many casualties (15 dead and 30 wounded) before finally withdrawing from the action. She was the only County class cruiser to undergo a major modernisation. The refit took place at Chatham 1939-41, and completely altered her original 3-funnel profile.

HMS Birmingham seen here at H Berth on the River Medway in the 1950's, after a two year major reconstruction at Portsmouth. On completion she sailed for the Far East, serving in the later stages of the Korean War. Shown to good effect in this picture is the unique profile of her bows. She was completed without the knuckle common in all British cruiser construction since the E class. There being no discernable advantage with the new design, it was intended that ***Birmingham*** be refitted with a standard knuckle, but the war intervened and she kept the flared bow throughout her service life.

The Great Sheers were a prominent landmark in the dockyard for over 80 years. At 140 feet high, they were erected alongside one basin in 1871 and were used for lifting heavy equipment such as gun turrets. Seen here in use during the construction of the battleship *Irresistible* at the turn of the century. They were eventually demolished in 1951.

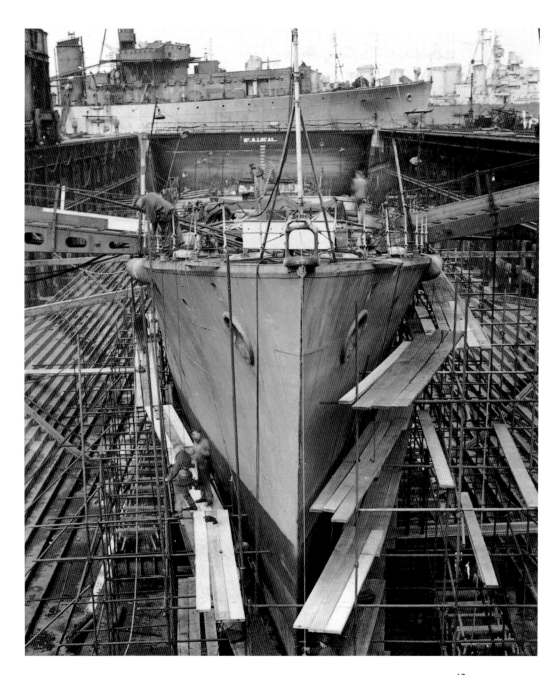

This photograph dated 1951 shows the early use of tubular staging in docks. The former Emergency War class destroyer *Virago*, seen here during her 1951-52 Type 15 frigate conversion in No. 6 Dock would have had to use wooden stages and platforms suspended with wires prior to this. The River class frigate visible in the basin beyond the dock is probably the *Plym*, which was refitted at Chatham from September 1951 to February 1952 prior to being expended on trials of the atomic bomb.

HMS Virago leaves 2 basin after her substantial reconstruction as an anti-submarine frigate in 1952. Built as a V Class Destroyer in 1943 she initially served in the Far East. She is credited, with her sister V Class ships (***Venus***, ***Verulam*** and ***Vigilant*** together with ***Saumarez***), of sinking the Japanese heavy cruiser ***Haguro*** in May 1945. Following conversion, ***Virago*** served with the 6th Frigate Squadron from 1953-54, followed by a period in reserve at Chatham (1955-60). After a short period of service with the 17th Frigate Squadron in the early 1960's she was once more reduced to reserve, this time at Devonport (1963-64). She arrived at Faslane on 4 June 1965 for breaking up. To the right of the picture can be seen two frigates (***Loch Alvie*** and ***Loch Fyne***) in care and maintenance awaiting modernisation.

HMS Campania (seen here in 1952) being towed between basins on her way to No 9 Dock to be fitted out as flagship for the first British nuclear tests at Monte Bello Islands. Built as a refrigerated cargo ship for the Shaw Saville Line in 1941 she was taken over by the RN and converted to an Escort Carrier. She was launched in 1943 and completed in March 1944. She saw war service mainly in the Arctic, her aircraft sinking ***U-921*** and ***U-365***. Post 1945 her role was that of an aircraft ferry and transport ship. In 1951 she was fitted out as a mobile exhibition centre for the Festival of Britain and toured the country that year bringing highlights of the festival to those who could not get to London. ***Campania*** was eventually scrapped at Blyth in 1955. A gathering of Algerine class minesweepers can be seen to the left (note the sailor in the yards enjoying a birds eye view of proceedings).

HMS Superb was built as a Minotaur Class (Second Batch) Cruiser, the only one to be completed and, together with her near sister ***Swiftsure***, was the most modern cruiser in the post war fleet, seeing extensive service. The remainder of the class, due to the ending of the war, were laid up until 1955 when it was decided to complete them as the Tiger Class vessels. Seen here leaving three basin in 1952 as the Flagship of Flag Officer Flotillas. She was eventually scrapped at Dalmiur in 1960.

HMS Shackelton in August 1953 after her conversion to a survey ship. Built in 1936 as a minesweeper she was launched at Devonport on 10 December 1936 as ***Sharpshooter***. In 1942 she sank ***U-655*** by ramming in the Arctic. She was converted for survey duties in 1945 and renamed in 1953. She carried out survey duties in the far East 1946-48, and then in Home Waters until 1962, when she paid off. She was broken up in 1965. The aircraft carrier ahead is thought to be ***Campania***.

The Colony class cruiser **HMS Jamaica** berthed at Farewell Corner during Navy Days 1955. Completed in 1942, she remained in the Home Fleet during the war years, mainly escorting Russian Convoys which included action against the **Hipper** and **Scharnhorst**. In 1949 a deployment to the West Indies was cut short when she was sent to the Far East as a result of the Yangtse incident. She remained there until 1951 seeing action off Korea. Paid off in 1957 she was scrapped at Dalmuir in 1960.
(Bill Rice)

HMS Sheffield, photographed during her extensive refit in 1950, was launched in 1936. She served in the Home and Mediterranean Fleets throughout the war, taking part in some of the major sea engagements including the sinking of the German battleships **Bismarck** (where **Sheffield** herself mistakenly became the target for an aerial torpedo strike from **Ark Royal's** Swordfish) and **Scharnhorst**. Her battle honours read like a Who's Who of the great naval campaigns of WWII; Norway 1940; Spartivento 1940; Atlantic 1941-43; Bismarck Action 1941; Mediterranean 1941; Malta Convoys 1941; Arctic 1941-43; North Africa 1942; Barents Sea 1942; Salerno 1943; Biscay 1943 and North Cape 1943. She was broken up at Faslane in 1967.

(Ben Newton)

The Battle class destroyer **HMS Aisne,** seen here in July 1957, moored off Thunderbolt Pier, near the No. 2 covered slip (which burnt down in 1966) was built by Vickers-Armstrong, launched in 1945 and completed in March 1947. Placed in reserve in 1950 at Chatham, she became Living Ship for **HMS Neptune** (the name of the Reserve Fleet at Chatham). Brought out of reserve in the late fifties she underwent a major conversion to a radar picket destroyer, which was completed in 1962. Paid off, she arrived at Inverkeithing in June 1970 to be broken up.

TID 97 was one of 182 TID Class small tugs built between 1945/1946 for the Ministry of War Transport. They were not built exclusively for RN use but as a wartime measure to replace lost commercial vessels and to provide vessels suitable to support impending invasion preparations. The origin of the TID abbreviation remains controversial with interpretations varying from Tug Invasion Duty, to Tug Intermediate Design to Tiddler. Many were lost in action in the last months of the war. On 29 December 1962 ***TID 97*** was working in 3 basin mooring ***RFA Hebe*** in bad weather when ***Hebe's*** wash overwhelmed her and she sank with the loss of three crewmen. This photograph shows her being raised by the Salvage Vessel ***Swin*** on 4 January 1963.

The veteran Submarine Depot Ship **HMS Forth** is seen here at Chatham during her 1962/1966 reconstruction to enable her to support nuclear powered submarines. Originally launched on 11 August 1938 the ship had seen war service in support of the Second and Third Submarine Flotillas, crossing the Atlantic in 1941 to support submarines operating from Halifax, Nova Scotia. After the war she operated in the Mediterranean and later took part in the Suez operations. She returned to Devonport in 1960, after 12 years operating in the Mediterranean. After five years based in Singapore, supporting the Seventh Submarine Squadron, she returned to Devonport in 1971 where she was renamed **Defiance**. Placed on the disposal list in 1978 she eventually returned to the Medway in 1985 to be broken up.

Mary the horse that pulled the Barrack's dustcart for many years, marches past Commander, later Rear Admiral, D W Haslam OBE on divisions for the last time. Saved from the knacker's yard by money raised by the Ships Company she left Chatham after this parade for a retirement home.

RFA Bacchus, one of a class of two store carriers built by Henry Robb and Co Ltd at Leith. Launched in June and completed in September 1962 for the British India Steam Navigation Co. She was taken over by the MoD on a long bareboat charter and operated as an RFA, together with her sistership ***Hebe***, to serve as a stores freighter running between Chatham and Singapore, via Gibraltar, Malta and Aden. In 1973 she was purchased by P&O but remained on charter. She was sold in 1981.

The RMAS Tug **Expeller**, seen here in 1964 working on the River Medway, was originally built in Germany, by Nobiskrug GMBH in 1942, for the German Navy. Named **Bora** she was taken as a war prize and renamed **Expeller**, and worked either at Chatham or Portland thereafter. In 1967 she was replaced by the tug **Mastiff** and sold to Salvatori Bezzina, Malta for further service as **Sabi**.

The Inshore Survey Squadron, comprising **HM Ships Egeria**, **Echo** and **Enterprise** undergo a "squadron docking period". They were all built and launched between 1957 and 1958 by different builders, **Echo** by Samuel White at Cowes, **Egeria** by William Weatherhead at Cockenzie and **Enterprise** by M W Blackmore at Bideford. The squadron was tasked to carry out surveys of UK coastal waters. Fitted with modern radar, echo sounders and asdic for bottom searches and wreck location all three vessels surveyed many thousands of miles of the coast and seabed during their lives. In time of war they could be quickly converted to armed inshore minesweepers, a class they closely resembled, by the addition of a 40mm Bofors on the forecastle and sweepgear aft. In 1986 **Egeria** was loaned to the Marine Society. **Enterprise** was sold to the society as spares for **Echo** which also had been sold to the Society and renamed **Earl of Romney**.

Photographed shortly after her launch on 25 September 1965, **HMCS Onondaga** was one of three Oberons (**Ojibwa** and **Okanagan** being the other two) built for Canada, and to Canadian specifications. Based on the British Oberon class, there were some design changes to meet specific needs. These modifications included the installation of Canadian communication systems and increased air-conditioning to meet the extremes of climate in the Canadian theatre of operations.

Tuesday 12 July 1966 dawned as any other day over the Dockyard. But, by the end of it a piece of history would lay in ashes. Built in 1813 No 2 Slip was 300 feet in length, 150 feet wide and rose to a height of 120 feet. Originally built during the time of wooden ships in the yard it could not handle the bigger and heavier ironclads and eventually the slip was filled in and the building became a store and a general building. At 1000 smoke and flames were seen by workers inside the building, the Dockyard fire brigade was called and by 1015 engines were racing to the dockyard from Maidstone and Gravesend. By 1020 smoke and flames were rising 300 feet into the air and could be seen as far away as Southend. By 1145 it was all over. After 153 years No 2 slip had been reduced to ashes.

The Type 61 Aircraft Direction frigate **HMS Llandaff** leaves Chatham in 1966 after undergoing an extensive modernisation refit. She completed seven commissions in the Home/Far East Fleets. On 10 December 1976 she was transferred to the Bangladeshi Navy, at a ceremony in London, being renamed **Umar Farooq**. Her pennant numbers were reversed in Bangladeshi service, to become F16. She was still in service in 2003.

The Royal Naval Supply & Transport Service was a little known, but very important civilian service unit. The RNSTS moved stores of all shapes and sizes around the world. This photograph taken on 21 July 1968 shows a Sea Vixen being unloaded from **RFA Robert Middleton** in three basin. The aircraft had been ferried from the Royal Naval Aircraft Yard at Fleetlands (Gosport). The aircraft was to be reloaded into **RFA Hebe** or **Bacchus** for onward shipping to Singapore and the Naval Air Holding Unit at RAF Changi. The barge is being handled by the tug **Collie.**

Gently does it... The same Sea Vixen (XN 692) is slowly manoeuvred out of the hold of the ***Robert Middleton***. Although the aircraft wings have been folded and the majority of the exposed working parts liberally sealed with protective polythene sheet, the nose mounted radar seems very vulnerable to damage!

The Army Landing Craft *Abbeville* arrives at Chatham on 23 October 1969 for repairs, after she was involved in a collision with a Dutch Motor Vessel off Cap Gris Nez in thick fog earlier that month. The Motor Vessel sank almost immediately with the loss of her cabin boy. *Abbeville* rescued eight members of the crew. On completion of repairs, costing an estimated £11,000, she returned to the 20th LTC Support Regiment Royal Corps of Transport at Gosport.

HMS Endurance was built in Denmark as the commercial ***MV Anita Dan*** in 1956/7; she was converted at Harland and Wolff in 1967 for Royal Naval service as an Ice Patrol Ship. Complete with red hull, white superstructure and buff funnel, she spent most of her life in Antarctica supporting the British Antarctic Survey. She was involved in the Falklands War and was due to be laid up prior to the conflict which then gave her an extended life. She was sold to Pakistan in 1993. She is seen here at Chatham open for Navy Days.

HMS Exmouth started life as a standard Type 14 frigate in 1957. After various roles as a submarine target ship, and in the Fishery Protection Squadron, she was taken to Chatham in 1966 for a two year conversion refit. She was to be used as a trials ship for gas turbines and was fitted with one Olympus and two Proteus gas turbines giving this single screw frigate a speed of 28 knots. The photograph shows her leaving Chatham in her new guise. Her enlarged funnel and extesive midships superstructure, housing the air intakes (necessary to feed the Gas Turbine's voracious appetite for air) and exhaust uptakes are evident in this photograph.

The Type 12 frigate **HMS Plymouth** seen here in February 1968 having her 4.5-inch Mk 6 turret re-installed. These turrets were refitted in the Weapons Equipment Shop and then transported around No1 Basin to the 120 ton crane on the north side. A set route was used - down Dock Head Road, right into West Road and around No9 Dock, into St Mary's Road onto North Side One. this operation was entrusted to such heavy haulage firms as Hallett and Silberman or Pickfords, using rear steering low-loaders. With the combined weight of the vehicle and turret being over 45 tons, many culverts running across the route had to be plated over with steel. The seemingly simple task of transporting a turret required co-ordination and planning across a wide spectrum of trades and departments - Bosun of the Yard, MoD Police, Boiler Makers, PSTO(N), Shipwrights, Weapons Fitters and more. The photograph shows the new turret being lowered into the deck ring. The items projecting below the turret are the shell and cordite hoists and the spent cartridge chamber. The final positioning operation warranted plenty of onlookers!

The coastal survey vessel **HMS Bulldog** enters the South Lock on a visit to Chatham. She was launched at Lowestoft in March 1968 and finally paid off in July 2001. In 1997 she was the first survey ship to act as the command ship of NATO's Standing Naval Force Channel. Over her bridge can be seen the three ships of the Inshore Survey Squadron moored at Gillingham Pier. To the right of the picture can be seen the entrance to the old Collier Wharf. Reportedly the best steaming coal would be unloaded here during the early 20th Century.

The Daring class destroyer **HMS Diamond** was completed by John Brown's, Clydebank, in February 1952, one of the last class of the traditional destroyers, powerfully armed with three twin 4.5-inch guns and ten torpedo tubes. In later years she was modernised with a reduced torpedo armament and improved gunnery fire control system but she still retained her graceful but formidable looks. Seen here leaving Chatham in October 1969 on her way to Portsmouth - and Fareham Creek, where she eventually became a Harbour Training Ship. She remained at Gosport until towed back to the Medway for breaking up in November 1981.

HMS Reward was a Bustler Class tug built by Henry Robb at Leith in 1944. Completely RN manned she spent two years at Chatham, being placed in a state of preservation in 1957. In 1958 she was transferred to reserve at Pembroke Dock. On 22 March 1960 she arrived at Malta (under tow of *Agile*) for service with the Target Squadron. By January 1962 she had returned to Chatham, via Gibraltar, and in May of that year was chartered to United Towing and renamed *Englishman.* She reverted to the RFA in 1963 when she again became *Reward*. She was once more taken over by the RN in 1975 for patrol duties in the UK offshore oilfields. However, her patrol career was to be short-lived as disaster struck on 10 August 1976 when she sank following a collision, in thick fog, with the German freighter *Plainsman* in the Firth of Forth. She was salvaged on 29 August by *Magnus III* and sold for scrap.

TS Arethusa was built by the Blohm and Voss shipyard Hamburg in 1911. She spent her early years in the nitrate trade, sailing around Cape Horn many times. In 1933 she was bought by the charity Shaftsbury Homes and for the next 40 years laid at Upnor as a training ship. Many of her boys achieved great things in life and some served with distinction in the RN. From 1940 until 1945 she served as an accommodation ship in Chatham and was renamed ***Pekin*** during this time. This photograph shows her being towed into the lock by the tugs ***Barbara*** and ***Collie*** for refit prior to going to the USA in August 1970 to be placed on public display.

HMS Triumph began her career as a light fleet carrier in 1946. After service as a trials and training carrier, she took part in operations off Malaya and then Korea. Early trials of the angled flight deck were carried out in 1953 before she became a Cadets Training Ship. After conversion to a Heavy Repair Ship at Portsmouth (as seen here) she was based at Singapore but returned to Chatham in 1972, paid off and lay in reserve until 1981, when she was towed to Spain and scrapped.

This fine photograph taken in 1972 shows the Dockyard's three basins and the naval barracks, **HMS Pembroke**, top right. The photo was taken during Navy Days. Ships present consist of the cruiser **HMS Blake** in one basin (bottom). **HMS Triumph** in three basin at the top. Two basin has vessels of the Standby Squadron on the left and various frigates and destroyers to the right. The Ice Patrol Ship **HMS Endurance** can be seen in the drydock at the top right hand corner of One Basin.

HMS Soberton, shown here in No. 2 Dock, nears the end of a 75-week refit in 1979. She had had extensive hull restoration, a new stem fitted and much of the upper deck planking renewed. For the first time in a refit ***Soberton*** was "cocooned" in plastic covers to allow all weather working. After trials, she joined the Fishery Protection Squadron, where she operated for 35 years continuously. She was used for Sea Cadet training in the 1990's and was broken up in 1998.

The WWII vintage destroyer **HMS Cavalier** is seen here at Chatham on 6 July 1972, the last day before her decommissioning. She was due to be sold for scrap until the Cavalier Trust raised enough money to buy her. She was towed from Chatham on 11 October 1977 and after a few days at Portsmouth was towed to Southampton on 21 October. After being placed on display firstly at Southampton and then at Brighton (both unsuccessful) she was eventually laid up at Hebburn. In 1998 she was brought back to Chatham and refurbished and is now (2003) a major attraction at the Historic Dockyard.

RMAS Kinloss stands guard over the wreck of the ammunition ship *Richard Montgomery* whilst RN and RMAS divers carry out their annual survey. The American vessel was carrying a 7000-ton cargo of ammunition when she ran aground off Sheerness in 1944 and broke her back. Half the cargo was removed at the time, the remainder was considered too dangerous to move. The survey covering the hull and the cargo is carried out annually, experts consider the ship to be safe and the intention is to leave her to break up in situ.

In 1972 it was announced that a third Oberon Class submarine was to be built for Brazil at Vickers. Named **Tonelero** completion was delayed by a serious fire on board originating in the electrical cabling. She was towed to Chatham in 1974 for repair and here we see an entire 60 foot centre section being replaced. This fire forced the decision to be made to replace all cabling in all Oberon's under construction . She eventually sailed for Brazil in 1978. She sank at her moorings in Guanabara Bay, Rio de Janiero on 24 December 2000. Salved later, she was deleted in 2001.

The Type 41 anti-aircraft frigate **HMS Leopard** makes a fine backdrop as British TV personality Monty Modlyn talks to the Port Admiral, Rear Admiral Bevan, about the role of the Naval base in peacetime. **Leopard** was laid up at the time, having arrived at Chatham to pay-off in January 1976. On 6 July 1977 she was sold to A. Howden and Co. for breaking up at nearby Dartford.

This excellent photograph of No2 and No3 Basins, the locks and the river at the top was taken at Navy Days 1975. The ships present were, starting clockwise in No3 basin (top), *Triumph*, *Finwhale*, *Gold Rover*, *Olympus*, *Tartar*, *Vos* and *Buyskes* of the Royal Netherlands Navy, *Fife* and *Plymouth*. In No2 Basin clockwise from the top right, *Londonderry*, *Lynx*, *Jaguar*, *TCV Caldy*, *Berry Head*, *Keppel*, *Cavalier* and *Rothesay*.

A rare sight in No.3 Basin - three Rover Class ships alongside at the same time. To the left **RFA Gold Rover,** in the centre **RFA Blue Rover** and **RFA Black Rover** to the right. All built in the late 1960s/early 1970's these small tankers supply oil, freshwater and limited dry goods under all conditions whilst underway. **RFA Blue Rover**, the only one of the class to have served in the Falklands War, was transferred to the Portuguese Navy in 1993 being renamed **Berrio**.

HMS *Killiecrankie* looking slightly dented after being in collision with the East German ship *Sirrah* off Sheerness. *Killiecrankie* had just finished an extended refit in Chatham and was on post refit trials when the collision occurred. She was completed in May 1954 as ***Bickington*** but by October that year had been renamed ***Curzon*** when attached to Sussex Division RNR. By 1960 she was attached to the Forth Division RNR based at Granton, assuming the name ***Killiecrankie***. She eventually returned to the RN and the Fishery Protection Squadron in 1976 and was able to assume her original name. She was broken up in 1988.

It was just like going back to Nelson's day at Bull Nose on 30 Noveber 1976. The hydraulic system failed, preventing the outer caisson of the north lock from closing-and it thus had to be closed by hand. Two teams of 40 labourers struggled to turn the capstan against a falling tide. The caisson was eventually closed after 95 minutes - all that was missing was the fiddler to keep them in time.

HMS Lincoln seen in reserve at Chatham as part of the Standby Squadron in 1979. The Squadron comprised ships at short notice for operational service, and replaced the old "Reserve Fleet". Completed in 1960 she was fitted with 12-foot controllable pitch propellers. She undertook Cod War patrols in 1973, and was in collision with the gunboat *Aegir* in July 1973 and again (twice) in September 1973 after which she had her bows and stern reinforced with concrete and an external wooden sheathing. She was broken up in 1983.

HMS Opossum, launched at Chatham in May 1963, is seen here being maneouvered into dock for refitting - it was to be the last conventional submarine refit to be carried out at Chatham, marking the end of a sixty year link between the Dockyard and the Navy's non nuclear-powered submarines. She was the last of her class to run in RN service, paying off in August 1993.

The Ton Class Minesweeper *HMS Stubbington,* having completed a 14 month refit, is seen here on 18 June 1977 at her Re-commissioning Ceremony. She was to join the Fishery Protection Squadron whose badge she is displaying on her funnel. Prior to her refit she had served as the Tay Division RNR ship, from 1972-76, bearing the name *Montrose*. She paid off in 1986 and was broken up 3 years later at Bilbao.

HM Dockyard Chatham in the 1970's. The Standby Squadron in No. 2 basin and *Triumph* in No.3 basin. Alas all now gone.

HM Dockyard Chatham, shown here in this 1970's aerial photograph, sits snugly in a bend of the River Medway. The top section shows St. Mary's Island stretching from the river to the basins. The buildings along the basin house the Fleet Maintenance Unit, the Small Craft Refit Group and many of the technical workshops run by the RN. Centre bottom are the locks leading into No.3 basin and thence to No.2 and No.1 basins. The left side shows the dockyard workshops, river docks, slipways and administration buildings. In the centre can be seen the accommodation blocks of **HMS Pembroke** - now the University of Greenwich.

This rare photograph of the nuclear powered submarine **HMS Courageous** was taken in July 1978 during her basin trials in No 1 Basin. Laid down in 1968 and launched in 1970 at Vickers she was commissioned in 1972 and attached to the Third Submarine Squadron. Paid off in 1992 she is now on display at Devonport Naval Base as part of a growing museum and visitor complex.

HMS Valiant is seen here re-entering the Nuclear Refit Complex, following her refit, to prepare for her post-refit trials. The complex is located to left of the picture. She paid off in August 1994 and was laid up at Devonport.

RFA Empire Gull undergoing refit in No 8 dry dock in 1975. Starting life in Canada as LST(3) 3523 in 1945, she was renamed **HMS Trouncer** in 1947 and **RFA Empire Gull** in 1956. She was the only LST ever operated by the RFA and was primarily used to transport non-perishable cargoes on the Marchwood to Antwerp run. Her black hull is a legacy of her civilian days operating under contract with British India Steam Navigation Company. She was withdrawn from service in 1978 and scrapped at Santander, Spain, in 1980.

The Type 12 frigate **HMS Yarmouth** looking the worse for wear arrived in South Lock on 15 March 1976 for repairs. During The her second Cod War Patrol she was in collision with the Icelandic Gunboats **Thor** (twice) and **Baldur** leaving her bows badly damaged. Comleted in 1960, **Yarmouth** was later converted to carry a helicopter. She took part in the Falklands War, 1982, and was expended as a target in 1987.

HMS Blake was laid down as one of the Swiftsure Class cruisers; these ships had a chequered building and conversion history extending over 30 years. Work commenced in 1942 and her launch took place at the end of WW2. Work was suspended in 1946, but resumed again in 1954. She was partially dismantled in 1955 preparatory to rebuilding to a revised design, and not completed until the 60's. Even then they only had a short life span as conventional "push-button" cruisers. In 1965 she was converted into a helicopter carrier, her original after 6-inch turret and superstructure being replaced by a huge hangar and flight deck, and commissioned as such in 1969. Seen here arriving in Chatham with a full complement of four Sea King ASW helicopters squeezed on deck.

HMS Blake is seen here arriving at Chatham in 1979, having been partially de-equipped, to be laid up prior to disposal. In October 1982 she was towed to Cairnryan to be broken up. The tug in the foreground, **RMAS Typhoon**, was completed in 1960 and designed for ocean towing, rescue, salvage and firefighting. In 1982 she sailed for the Falkland Islands with the Royal Naval Task Force.

HMS Valiant photographed here in No 6 dock in June 1979 halfway through a 2 year refit. Launched in 1963 and commissioned in July 1966 she immediately went to the Far East Fleet. The following year she made the return 12,000 mile journey from Singapore to the UK submerged - in 28 days.

HMS Nubian arrived at Chatham in January 1980 to join the Standby Squadron where she joined others of the class, **Eskimo**, **Gurkha**, **Zulu** and **Mohawk** for refit and repairs prior to laying up. The intention was that by laying up these vessels manpower could be released for new ships commissioning in 1980. Three of the class were placed on the disposal list in 1981, but in the aftermath of the Falklands War, **Zulu**, **Gurkha** and **Tartar** were recommissioned. **Eskimo**, **Nubian** and **Mohawk** were stripped of spares for the three active ships. By 1984 the three active ships had paid off and were transferred to Indonesia. The three remaining vessels were eventually scrapped or used as targets, **Nubian** being expended as a target in May 1987.

HMS Kent arrives at the locks on a visit to Chatham in 1980. Completed in August 1963, she carried out patrols in the Far East during Confrontation with Indonesia during her first commission. Returning to the UK ***Kent*** was the host ship at Gibraltar in 1968 during the talks on Southern Rhodesia's future. Paid off in 1980 she took up duties as a Harbour Training Ship in Portsmouth until 1993. After her training role in Portsmouth she was towed to India for breaking in November 1997.

HMS Churchill was the Navy's fourth Nuclear Fleet Submarine, and was completed by Vickers-Armstrong at Barrow on 15 July 1970. Of 4,400 tons she was considered very large by contemporary standards. Seen here in the Chatham Nuclear Refit Complex in 1981, the white structure towering over the shrouded hull is the Reactor Refuelling Housing.

HMS Triumph left Chatham on 9 December 1981 after nearly eight years in reserve. She had a varied career, first as an Aircraft Carrier then a Cadet Training Ship and finally as a Heavy Repair Ship supporting ships and submarines in the Far East. This last journey ended in Spain where she was broken up. If she had still been at Chatham at the outbreak of the Falklands War a year later she would doubtless have been pressed into service in the South Atlantic.

RMAS Mastiff seen here going astern into North Lock, was one of 19 Dog Class Tugs, small, powerful and very maneouverable Used as general duty tugs in HM Dockyards they were also fitted with firefighting and salvage equipment. She is pictured here in October 1976 on a day out on the river with a group of handicapped children from London.

HMS Endurance seen here returning from the Falklands in 1983. She was about to be withdrawn from service without replacement, an action many say precipitated events in the South Atlantic, when the Falklands War broke out. She remained in service until replaced by ***MV Polar Circle***, eventually being paid off in 1991 and sold to Pakistani interests.

Farewell Chatham.....The last ceremonial divisions in 1983. Compare this with the photograph on page 11.

HMS Hermoine, the last warship to be refitted at Chatham, is ceremonially escorted from the Dockyard, on 21 June 1983, by RMAS vessels. On 17 April 1984 the Dockyard was closed and re-opened as the Historic Dockyard the same day, thus ending nearly 450 years of service to the Royal Navy. ***Hermione*** was broken up in 1998.

A further photograph of **HMS Hermione** leaving Chatham on 21 June 1983. Leading the way down river is the Flag Officer Medway aboard his barge.

HMS Ocelot arrived at No. 2 Dock for refit in July 1992 prior to going on public exhibition as part of the Historic Dockyard. On completion she was moved next door to No. 3 Dock where she is on permanent display - and open to the public.

SUBMARINES BUILT AT CHATHAM

DESIGNATION		LENGTH EXTREME (FT — INS)	BREADTH EXTREME (FT — INS)	DISPT. TONS	LAID DOWN	LAUNCHED	COMPLETED
C	17	142 — 2	13 — 7	320	11 — 3 — 07	13 — 8 — 08	13 — 5 — 09
	18	,,	,,	,,	,,	10 — 10 — 08	23 — 7 — 09
	19	,,	,,	,,	1 — 6 — 08	20 — 3 — 09	9 — 11 — 09
	20	,,	,,	,,	,,	27 — 11 — 09	31 — 1 — 10
	33	,,	,,	,,	29 — 3 — 09	10 — 5 — 10	13 — 8 — 10
	34	,,	,,	,,	,,	8 — 6 — 10	17 — 9 — 10
D	7	168 — 0	20 — 6	612	14 — 2 — 10	14 — 1 — 11	14 — 12 — 11
	8	,,	,,	,,	,,	23 — 9 — 11	23 — 3 — 12
E	1	178 — 0	22 — 8½	793	14 — 2 — 11	9 — 11 — 12	30 — 4 — 13
	2	,,	,,	,,	,,	23 — 11 — 12	30 — 6 — 13
	7	,,	,,	788	30 — 3 — 12	2 — 10 — 13	14 — 3 — 14
	8	,,	,,	,,	,,	30 — 10 — 13	13 — 6 — 14
	12	,,	,,	798	16 — 12 — 12	5 — 9 — 14	14 — 10 — 14
	13	,,	,,	,,	,,	22 — 9 — 14	9 — 12 — 14
F	1	151 — 0	16 — 0¾	515	1 — 12 — 13	31 — 3 — 15	14 — 8 — 15
G	1	186 — 0	22 — 8	873	1 — 10 — 14	14 — 8 — 15	7 — 12 — 15
	2	,,	,,	,,	,,	23 — 12 — 15	18 — 3 — 16
	3	,,	,,	,,	,,	22 — 1 — 16	13 — 4 — 16
	4	,,	,,	,,	12 — 10 — 14	23 — 10 — 15	3 — 2 — 16
	5	,,	,,	,,	,,	23 — 11 — 15	26 — 2 — 16
R	1	164 — 0	15 — 7	400	4 — 2 — 17	25 — 4 — 18	5 — 4 — 19
	2	,,	,,	,,	,,	,,	,,
	3	,,	,,	,,	,,	,,	,,
	4	,,	,,	,,	,,	8 — 6 — 18	,,
X	1	363 — 6	30 — 5	2,528	1 — 11 — 21	16 — 6 — 23	23 — 9 — 25
OBERON		269 — 8	27 — 11½	1510	22 — 3 — 24	24 — 9 — 26	24 — 8 — 27
ODIN		283 — 5	29 — 10⅝	1763	23 — 6 — 27	5 — 5 — 28	4 — 3 — 30
PARTHIAN		289 — 1	,,	1765	30 — 6 — 28	22 — 6 — 29	3 — 1 — 31
RAINBOW		285 — 11	29 — 11⅝	,,	24 — 7 — 29	14 — 5 — 30	23 — 1 — 32
SWORDFISH		202 — 5	24 — 0	740	1 — 12 — 30	10 — 11 — 31	24 — 11 — 32
STURGEON		,,	,,	,,	1 — 1 — 31	8 — 1 — 32	25 — 2 — 33
SEAHORSE		,,	,,	,,	14 — 9 — 31	15 — 11 — 32	29 — 9 — 33
STARFISH		,,	,,	,,	26 — 9 — 31	14 — 3 — 33	27 — 10 — 33
SHARK		208 — 8	,,	770	12 — 6 — 33	31 — 5 — 34	31 — 12 — 34
SNAPPER		,,	,,	,,	18 — 9 — 33	25 — 10 — 34	14 — 6 — 35
GRAMPUS		293 — 0	25 — 6	1750	20 — 8 — 34	25 — 2 — 36	10 — 3 — 37
SUNFISH		208 — 8	24 — 0	770	22 — 7 — 35	30 — 9 — 36	2 — 7 — 37
STERLET		,,	,,	,,	14 — 7 — 36	22 — 9 — 37	6 — 4 — 38
SEAL		293 — 0	25 — 6	1750	9 — 12 — 36	27 — 9 — 38	24 — 5 — 39
TIGRIS		275 — 0	26 — 7	1330	11 — 5 — 38	31 — 10 — 39	21 — 6 — 40
TORBAY		,,	,,	1325	21 — 11 — 38	9 — 4 — 40	14 — 1 — 41
UMPIRE		196 — 9¾	16 — 1	630	1 — 1 — 40	30 — 12 — 40	14 — 7 — 41
UNA		,,	,,	,,	7 — 5 — 40	10 — 6 — 41	29 — 9 — 41
SPLENDID		217 — 0	23 — 8	802	7 — 3 — 41	19 — 1 — 42	11 — 8 — 42
SPORTSMAN		,,	,,	,,	1 — 7 — 41	17 — 4 — 42	21 — 12 — 42
P242. SHALIMAR		,,	,,	,,	17 — 4 — 42	22 — 4 — 43	2 — 4 — 44
TRADEWIND		273 — 5¾	26 — 6	1320	11 — 2 — 42	11 — 12 — 42	25 — 9 — 43
TRENCHANT		,,	,,	,,	9 — 5 — 42	24 — 3 — 43	29 — 1 — 44
TURPIN		,,	,,	,,	24 — 5 — 43	5 — 8 — 44	20 — 11 — 44
THERMOPYLÆ		,,	,,	,,	26 — 10 — 43	27 — 6 — 45	15 — 12 — 45
ACHERON		279 — 3	22 — 3	1375	26 — 8 — 44	25 — 3 — 47	17 — 4 — 48
OBERON		295 — 3	26 — 6⅛	2200	28 — 11 — 57	18 — 7 — 59	23 — 2 — 61
ONSLAUGHT		,,	,,	,,	8 — 4 — 59	24 — 9 — 60	1 — 8 — 62
OCELOT		,,	,,	,,	17 — 11 — 60	5 — 5 — 62	20 — 1 — 64
OJIBWA		,,	,,	,,	27 — 9 — 62	29 — 2 — 64	14 — 9 — 65
ONONDAGA		,,	,,	,,	18 — 6 — 64	25 — 9 — 65	22 — 6 — 67
OKANAGAN		,,	,,	,,	25 — 3 — 65	17 — 9 — 66	22 — 6 — 68

Submarines were built at Chatham for 61 years. This board, now on display in the Chatham Historic Dockyard, lists all 57 submarines that were built at the yard.

The Main Gate of **HMS Pembroke**, through which generations of sailors have passed, still stands proudly today, 100 years after they were built. After the Barracks closed the University of Greenwich took over the site; visitors can still walk along the Main Road and recall past memories as little has outwardly changed.

Index